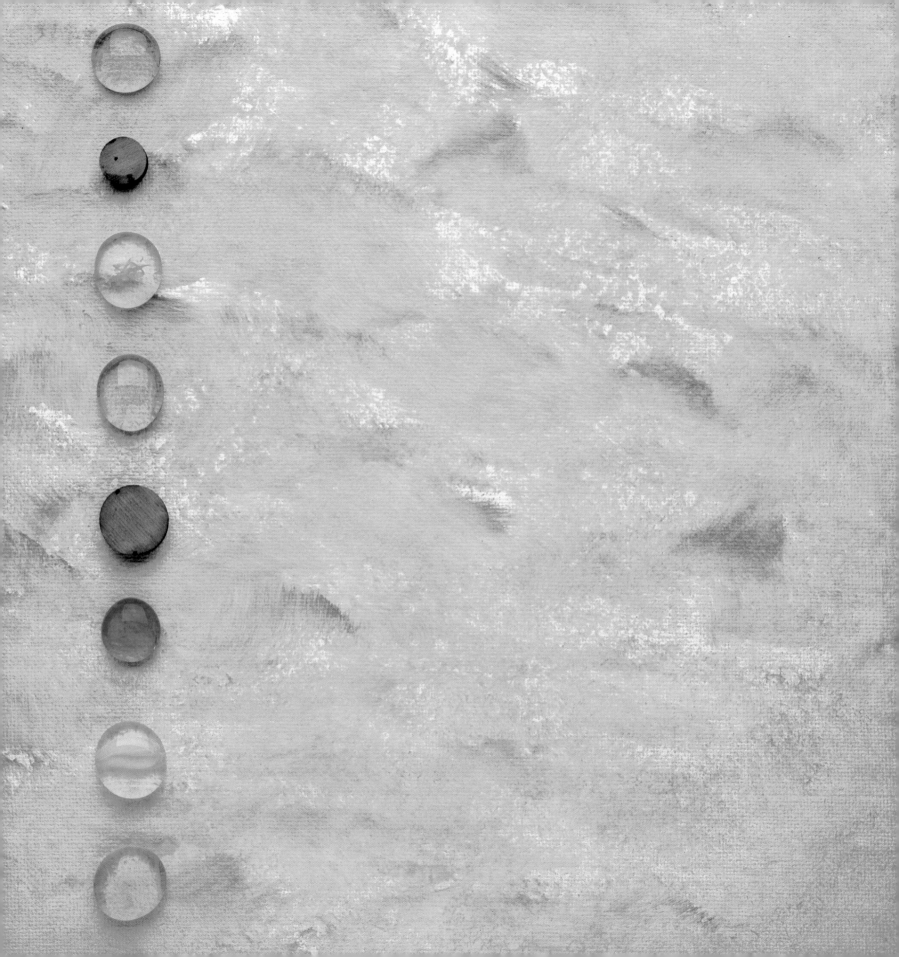

PICTURING GOD

by Ruth Goring

beaming
books
MINNEAPOLIS

For Deb, Rebecca, and the two Cindys

*And continually the soul does what it was made for:
it perceives God, it contemplates God, and it loves God.*

—Julian of Norwich

Copyright © 2019 Ruth Goring

Published in 2019 by Beaming Books, an imprint of 1517 Media. All rights reserved. No part of this book may be reproduced without the written permission of the publisher. Email copyright@1517.media. Printed in the United States of America.

25 24 23 22 21 20 19   1 2 3 4 5 6 7 8

ISBN: 978-1-5064-4939-5

Written and illustrated by Ruth Goring
Cover designed by Collaborate, Inc.
Interior designed by Tory Herman, 1517 Media
Photography by Michael Bracey
Author portrait by Katherine Vincent Lamb

Library of Congress Cataloging-in-Publication Data
Names: Goring, Ruth, author.
Title: Picturing God / by Ruth Goring.
Description: Minneapolis, MN : Beaming Books, 2019. | Audience: Ages 4-8.
Identifiers: LCCN 2019004267 | ISBN 9781506449395 (hardcover : alk. paper)
Subjects: LCSH: God (Christianity)--Juvenile literature. | God (Christianity)--Art--Juvenile literature.
Classification: LCC BT107 .G67 2019 | DDC 231/.4--dc23
LC record available at https://lccn.loc.gov/2019004267

VN0004589;9781506449395;AUG2019

Beaming Books
510 Marquette Avenue
Minneapolis, MN 55402
Beamingbooks.com

God is the Word,
and that Word is Love.

God is the Light of the world
that shines in every darkness—

the beautiful darkness of night,

the darkness of hiding
when we are afraid,

the deep darkness
of being all alone.

God shines there.

When we don't know where to go,
God's light shines on our path

and leads us home.

God is our sunshine,
and we sprout like seeds,
open to the light, and
start to grow.

God's Living Water rains down from heaven to water our thirsty hearts.

God's love pours over us and never stops.

Living Water baptizes us,
saying, "You belong."

Jesus says,
"I am the Vine
and you are the branches."

We grow from God's Vine.
God's love flows through us
like juicy sap,

and then good things grow from us—

love and joy and peace,
like fat, mouth-watering grapes.

God is the Bread of Life
that feeds us and fills us up.

It is God's own life
given for us.

The Bread of Life
makes us strong—

strong enough to share,
strong enough to be kind,
strong enough for pure delight—

and we find new ways
to give God's love away.

God's goodness is like bright clothes
we can put on every morning,
with faith as a button
and peace as the sleeves.

When we are in danger,
Jesus is the Door
that opens to give
us shelter

and closes to keep us safe.

When we journey into places
that are slippery and scary,
our Shepherd stays close

Sometimes we must walk
in hot, dry deserts.

Then God is our Rock,

providing shade
and a place to rest.

God's Spirit is Wind,

blowing away our fear
and our mean words,

blowing in cheerfulness
and making us new.

The Spirit is our Comforter,
nearer than breath,

teaching us what we need to know,
wrapping us in love.

God is a Father who forgives
again and again,

who watches for us
and runs to meet us.

God is a Mother
who covers us with her wings.

Jesus himself is the Way we walk
to God–who is our Home.

Images of God in the Bible

The Bible is rich in metaphors for God—word-pictures that wake up our imaginations to God's greatness, wisdom, and love. This book is not nearly big enough to include all of them! Symbols like these feed our hearts, whether we are very young, very old, or somewhere in between.

Word
John 1:1–3

Love
1 John 4:7–8, 16

Light of the World
Psalm 104:1–2
John 1:4–10
John 8:12
Ephesians 5:8–9, 13–14

Living Water
Psalm 104:10–13
John 4:10–14
John 7:37–39

Vine
John 15:1–8

Bread of Life
Exodus 16:1–5, 14–18
John 6:35, 48–51

Clothing; Putting On Christ
Romans 13:14
Galatians 3:26–27

Door
John 10:7–10

Good Shepherd
Psalm 23
Luke 15:1–7
John 10:1–16

Rock
1 Samuel 2:2
Psalm 18:31
Psalm 95:1

Wind
Genesis 1:1–2
John 3:8

Comforter
Isaiah 66:13
John 14:16–18, 26

Father
Psalm 103:8, 13–14
Matthew 7:9–11
Luke 15:11–32

Mother
Deuteronomy 32:11–12, 18
Isaiah 42:14
Isaiah 49:15
Isaiah 66:13
Matthew 23:37
Luke 13:34

The Way
John 14:1–7

Home
2 Corinthians 5:1, 8
Psalm 84:3
John 14:23
Revelation 21:3

Ruth Goring is a poet, visual artist, and book editor who grew up in Colombia. Her first picture book was *Adriana's Angels* (Sparkhouse Family), published in Spanish as *Los Ángeles de Adriana*, which won a silver Moonbeam Award. Other publications include two books of poetry, *Soap Is Political* (Glass Lyre) and *Yellow Doors* (WordFarm), and several Bible study guides, including *Heart Renewal* (WaterBrook) and *Singleness* (InterVarsity Press).